SUPERSTARS OF THE
WNBA FINALS

by Brendan Flynn

Cody Koala

An Imprint of Pop!
popbooksonline.com

abdopublishing.com
Published by Pop!, a division of ABDO, PO Box 398166, Minneapolis,
Minnesota 55439. Copyright © 2019 by POP, LLC. International copyrights
reserved in all countries. No part of this book may be reproduced in any
form without written permission from the publisher. Pop!™ is a trademark
and logo of POP, LLC.

Printed in the United States of America, North Mankato, Minnesota

042018
092018

THIS BOOK CONTAINS
RECYCLED MATERIALS

Cover Photo: Stacy Bengs/AP Images
Interior Photos: Stacy Bengs/AP Images, 1, 7, 21 (top); Shutterstock Images, 5
(top); Aaron Lavinsky/Star Tribune/AP Images, 5 (bottom left); 8; Jim Mone/
AP Images, 5 (bottom right); Mark J. Terrill/AP Images, 11, 12, 19; Rick Scuteri/
AP Images, 15, 21 (bottom); Kamil Krzaczynski/AP Images, 17

Editor: Meg Gaertner
Series Designer: Laura Mitchell

Library of Congress Control Number: 2017963426
Publisher's Cataloging-in-Publication Data
Names: Flynn, Brendan, author.
Title: Superstars of the WNBA finals / by Brendan Flynn.
Description: Minneapolis, Minnesota : Pop!, 2019. | Series: Sports' greatest
    superstars | Includes online resources and index.
Identifiers: ISBN 9781532160349 (lib.bdg.) | ISBN 9781532161469 (ebook) |
Subjects: LCSH: Women basketball players--United States--Juvenile
    literature. | Sports records--Juvenile literature. | Women's National
    Basketball Association--Juvenile literature.
Classification: DDC 796.32364--dc23

Hello! My name is

Cody Koala

Pop open this book and you'll find QR codes like this one, loaded with information, so you can learn even more!

Scan this code* and others like it while you read,

or visit the website below to make this book pop.

popbooksonline.com/superstars-wnba-finals

*Scanning QR codes requires a web-enabled smart device with a QR code reader app and a camera.

Table of Contents

Chapter 1

Maya Moore in the WNBA Finals

The Women's National Basketball Association (WNBA) holds its Finals every fall.

Watch a video here!

The best players stand out as they help their team win.

Maya Moore plays for the Minnesota Lynx. Her team counts on her to make tough **shots** during big games. At the 2017 Finals, Moore did just that.

The Lynx had only 30 seconds to keep their small lead. Moore **dribbled** past the other team and jumped for a long shot. She scored! The Lynx won again.

Chapter 2

Candace Parker

Candace Parker is tall enough to be a **center**. But the Los Angeles Sparks star plays like a **guard**. She dribbles and passes to help her teammates.

Learn more here!

Parker can score points, too. At the 2016 Finals, she scored in the last minute to put her team ahead by one point. The Sparks won the Finals!

Parker was just the second WNBA player to dunk in a game.

Chapter 3

Diana Taurasi

Diana Taurasi plays for the Phoenix Mercury. She led her team to championships in 2007, 2009, and 2014. She scores a lot and she is very fast.

Complete an activity here!

Taurasi is a hard player to guard. Stand too close and she will dribble right past. But back off too much and she will make a long shot.

Taurasi won six championships while playing in Russia during the WNBA's off-season.

Chapter 4

Sylvia Fowles

Lynx center Sylvia Fowles is known for grabbing **rebounds**. If a shot is missed, Fowles will often get to the ball first. Her rebounds help the Lynx win.

Learn more here!

Fowles had 20 rebounds in Game 5 of the 2017 Finals. No player has ever had more in a WNBA Finals game.

Tamika Catchings, one of the best players in WNBA history, wins her first Finals in her 11th season with the Indiana Fever.

The Houston Comets win their fourth straight WNBA Finals.

Maya Moore and the Minnesota Lynx win their fourth WNBA Finals in seven years.

2000　　　　　**2012**　　　　　**2017**

2002　　　　　**2014**

Lisa Leslie leads the Los Angeles Sparks to their second straight WNBA Finals win.

Diana Taurasi wins the WNBA Finals Most Valuable Player Award as she leads the Phoenix Mercury to their third Finals win in eight years.

Making Connections

Text-to-Self

Does your school have a basketball team? Would you ever want to play on one? Why or why not?

Text-to-Text

Have you read about any other great sports players? What makes them great?

Text-to-World

Why do you think basketball is so popular around the world?

Glossary

center – a tall player who usually stands close to the basket.

dribble – to bounce the ball, usually while moving toward the basket.

guard – a player who handles the ball most of the time.

rebound – to grab the ball after a missed shot.

shot an attempt to score a basket.

Index

Online Resources

popbooksonline.com

Thanks for reading this Cody Koala book!

Scan this code* and others like it in this book, or visit the website below to make this book pop!

popbooksonline.com/superstars-wnba-finals

*Scanning QR codes requires a web-enabled smart device with a QR code reader app and a camera.